This book belongs to _____

Journal for the year_____

Home or Location _____

The Mary Engelbreit
Gardener's Journal

Illustrated by
Mary Engelbreit

Andrews and McMeel
A Universal Press Syndicate Company
Kansas City

® is a registered trademark of Mary Engelbreit Enterprises, Inc.

ISBN: 0-8362-4620-9

The Mary Engelbreit
Gardener's Journal

HURT NOT THE EARTH, NEITHER THE SEA, NOR THE TREES

REVELATIONS 7:3

Contents

How to Use This Book	8
Taking Stock	10
Climate & Conditions	11
Current Garden Grid	12
Future Plans	14
Future Plans Grid	16
Detailed Plans & Grids	18
Before & After Photos	26
Monthly Summary	31
Plantings Record	83
Other People's Gardens	102
Reference	104
Supplier Names	110
Notes	112

How to Use This Book

T he simultaneous joy and frustration of the garden is that it is never finished. Even when the last weed has been banished to the compost heap, rose bushes have been impeccably pruned, poppies and mums are blooming large and fragrantly, and tomatoes hang plump and ripe from the vine, a garden is always a work in progress.

True garden artists are never content. They are constantly refining, rethinking, and reinventing. And every spring, the creative process begins anew. A flat brown canvas lies in front of you, awaiting your bold strokes of color and your fine attention to detail; waiting to be brought to life by your unique vision. Paint it with white lilies, yellow narcissus, firecracker-red zinnias, or a thousand other colors from your *living* palette. Your work of art is never quite complete.

That's why this book should be your constant companion in the garden. The *Gardener's Journal* is divided into several different sections designed to help you record and organize information that will aid in your pursuit of the perfect garden in this year and years to come. A brief introduction to these sections follows.

Taking Stock This section will help you understand your growing environment and give you a permanent record of the current contents of your garden. Taking Stock is composed of two parts: Climate & Conditions and the Current Garden Grid. If you're not familiar with weather patterns and soil conditions in your area, completing the Climate & Conditions section should be an invaluable exercise. The Garden Grid section will give you a detailed and objective representation of your landscape and should be retained as a reference as your garden undergoes inevitable improvements and face-lifts in coming seasons.

Future Plans This section provides ample space for writing down ideas, plants to buy, and tasks to be completed. A large grid for overall planning and four smaller "detail" grids are also included.

Before & After Photos Photographing your garden at different stages of growth and at different times of the year gives you permanent reminders of your progress and success. This section is designed to accommodate garden photos for reference or pleasant remembrance.

Monthly Summary This important section lets you record your gardening progress throughout the year and offers helpful tips along the way. It will be an excellent reference and source of comparison in years to come.

Records The greater the variety of flowers, trees, shrubs and plants in your landscape or garden, the more exciting—and more complicated—it becomes. The Records section will help you keep track of your garden's contents as they become more diverse.

Other People's Gardens Good gardeners are always on the lookout for new arrangements, combinations, and layouts. Whether they come from a botanical garden, a neighbor's backyard, or a flower show, ideas that you'd like to duplicate should be recorded in this section.

Reference The final part of the *Gardener's Journal* contains helpful reference information, climate charts, and space for you to record the names, addresses, and phone numbers of important garden suppliers.

Every gardener knows that you get out of a garden just what you put into it. The same holds true for this journal. Fill it up with your thoughts, plans, projects, and results, and you'll reap sweet rewards for your efforts. Happy gardening!

Taking Stock

The following pages will help you determine and record the physical characteristics of your landscape and your overall growing conditions. Begin by completing the Climate & Conditions page opposite this one. If you can't complete this section on your own, check the reference section of your local library or ask your county agricultural extension office or local nursery professionals for help.

To use the Garden Grid section, begin by measuring your property. You will want to draw your landscape to scale, so once you have measured, select a scale ratio that will allow your entire property to fit on the grid. (Example: One square on the grid = five square feet.) Sketch in pencil and do a rough draft of your plan on tracing paper before putting it in your journal.

Once you've indicated your property's borders, sketch in the physical features of your property. Include your house, tool shed, pool, deck, and any other buildings or structures. Also indicate approximate height which will influence how much shade each structure will cast. Next, sketch in patios, walkways, outdoor faucets, electrical outlets, fences, walls, birdbaths, and other adornments.

After all of the non-organic features have been included, it's time to fill in your grid with trees, shrubs, hedges (record height of these also), garden plots, flower beds, and borders. Once these basic features are recorded, indicate, in detail, the position and type of plants in your garden and flower beds.

The most critical requirement of nearly all plants is sunlight. Consider using colored pencils to shade in areas of intense sun, partial shade, and total shade. Also indicate soil conditions, including makeup (rocky, sandy, clayey, organically rich, etc.) and drainage.

Remember, this grid is a snapshot of your garden as it currently exists. Following this section, other grids and lined pages are provided to indicate future plans.

Climate & Conditions

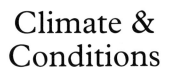

Property

Overall dimensions

Terrain type

Soil conditions

Climate:
    Average growing season
    Average last frost
    Average first frost
    Hardiness zone
    Yearly rainfall

Noteworthy conditions:
    Insects/pests
    Diseases

Drainage

Miscellaneous comments

Current Garden

Future Plans

Plants to buy
Clippings
Landscape changes
Goals for this year

Future Plans

Detailed Plans

Detailed plan for _____

Location _____

Dimensions _____

Hours of sunlight _____

Exposure _____

Soil conditions:

   Content/type _____

   Drainage _____

   pH level _____

   Slope _____

   Proximity of other plants _____

   Actions necessary to improve soil _____

_____

_____

Overall planting strategy _____

_____

_____

_____

Plants needed _____

_____

_____

Care:

   Watering _____

   Feeding _____

   Weed/pest control _____

   Pruning _____

   Miscellaneous _____

_____

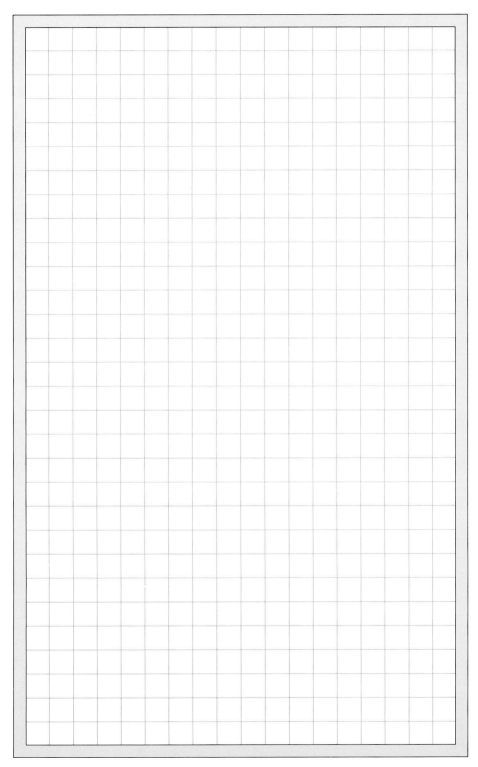

Detailed Plans

Detailed plan for _____

Location _____

Dimensions _____

Hours of sunlight _____

Exposure _____

Soil conditions:

    Content/type _____

    Drainage _____

    pH level _____

    Slope _____

    Proximity of other plants _____

    Actions necessary to improve soil _____

_____

Overall planting strategy _____

_____

_____

Plants needed _____

_____

_____

Care:

    Watering _____

    Feeding _____

    Weed/pest control _____

    Pruning _____

    Miscellaneous _____

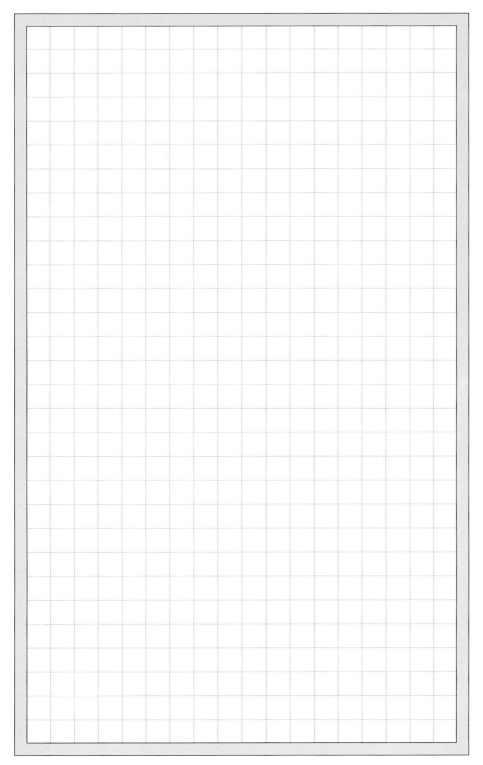

Detailed Plans

Detailed plan for _____

Location _____

Dimensions _____

Hours of sunlight _____

Exposure _____

Soil conditions:

    Content/type _____

    Drainage _____

    pH level _____

    Slope _____

    Proximity of other plants _____

    Actions necessary to improve soil _____

_____

Overall planting strategy _____

_____

_____

Plants needed _____

_____

_____

Care:

    Watering _____

    Feeding _____

    Weed/pest control _____

    Pruning _____

    Miscellaneous _____

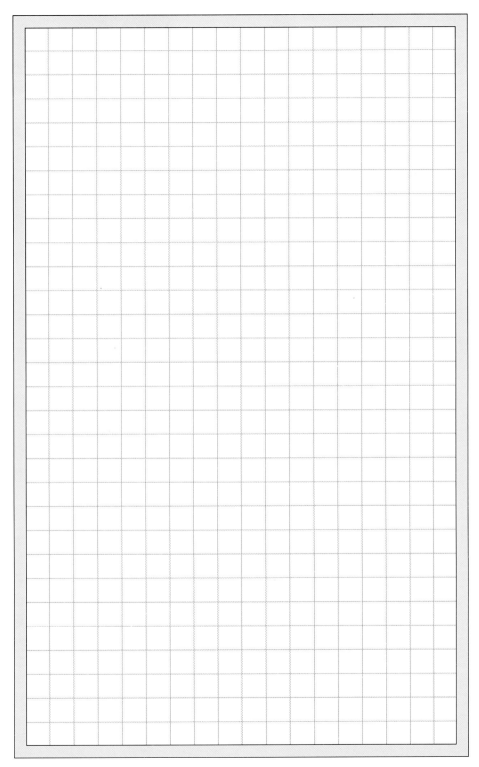

Detailed Plans

Detailed plan for _____

Location _____

Dimensions _____

Hours of sunlight _____

Exposure _____

Soil conditions:

  Content/type _____

  Drainage _____

  pH level _____

  Slope _____

  Proximity of other plants _____

  Actions necessary to improve soil _____

_____

_____

Overall planting strategy _____

_____

_____

_____

Plants needed _____

_____

_____

_____

Care:

  Watering _____

  Feeding _____

  Weed/pest control _____

  Pruning _____

  Miscellaneous _____

_____

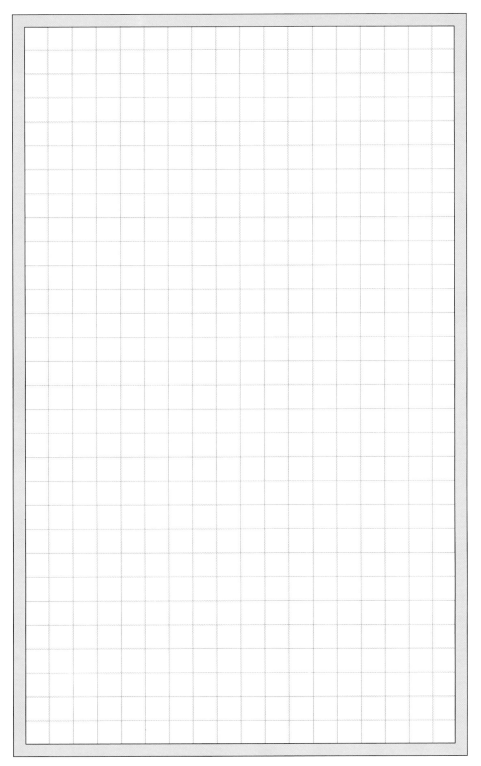

Before &
After Photos

Before &
After Photos

COME FORTH
INTO THE LIGHT
of THINGS,
LET NATURE
BE YOUR TEACHER
WILLIAM WORDSWORTH

Monthly Summary

Gardening gives us the unique opportunity to observe and support the wondrous lifecycle of plants. From a tiny seed full of promise and mystery to a fragile seedling; through glorious bloom and generation of new seeds, the cycle continues. The garden teaches us an annual lesson—that after even the harshest, most lifeless winter, spring will soon arrive, bringing renewal and rebirth.

To keep track of this glorious cycle of life, use the 12-Month Summary and the individual Monthly Summary sections that follow. The 12-Month Summary section provides a place to record thoughts about your garden's overall performance last year, climatic conditions for your area, improvements you'd like to make this year, and general thoughts about your garden.

Use the Monthly Summaries as you move through the year, recording the dates and conditions under which you sow seeds, cultivate the earth, transplant seedlings, feed and fertilize plants, and prune shrubs. Use this section to track blossom and harvest dates and results. Jot down methods and strategies that prove successful as well as mistakes that you don't want to make again.

Also use the Monthly Summary sections to record chores and activities that need to be completed. At the beginning of each monthly section, there is a listing of tasks that are likely to need attention during that particular month. Track your progress in completing these chores, but don't limit your comments to these areas. You can also use these sections to record random ideas, visitor comments, rainfall amounts, temperatures, and anything else you may want to reference in upcoming months or years.

12-Month Summary

Weather
Wildlife
Tips to remember
Accomplishments
Improvements

January

Despite steel-hard soil and frigid temperatures, your garden will be at its colorful, glorious peak this month—because January is a time for dreaming. With an anxious eye toward warmer days, smart gardeners are busy planning, sketching, reading, and ordering. With seed catalogs and garden magazines at hand, select vegetables and flowers for your garden. Pay special attention to the particular climate needs of plants. Choose proven performers for your area, but experiment with a few plants that won't show up in everyone else's yard.

In southern parts of the country, now is a good time to plant trees and shrubs. After planting, wrap the trunks with burlap to prevent sun and wind burn.

Week 1

Ordering
Sowing
Planting
Watering
Maintenance

Week 2

January

Tip: Take inventory of your tools and sharpen and repair those that need it. Rub linseed oil or furniture wax into wooden handles to give them a protective coating and reduce splintering.

January

Tip: Heavy, wet snow can damage branches of trees and shrubs. Knock the snow off of branches with a broom or mop.

Week 3

January

Week 4

Tip: If you live in a snowy climate, instead of using salt to melt snow and ice on walkways adjacent to plant or flower beds, try sprinkling on a chemical fertilizer, sand, or sawdust instead.

February

If you plan to sow your plants from seed, and your target date for outdoor planting is May 1, you'll need to start some varieties in February. Petunias, snapdragons, impatiens, wax begonias and geraniums are among those that require a long growing season (8 - 12 weeks) before they become large and strong enough to move outside. Remember, garden lore holds that seeds should be sown and transplanted only when the moon is waxing, never when it is waning.

Take advantage of February's occasional warm, spring-like day to prune late-summer blooming trees and shrubs. Do not prune spring-flowering trees at this time. Wait until you've enjoyed their spring display.

SOW GOOD SERVICES;
SWEET REMEMBRANCES
WILL GROW FROM THEM.
Mde. de Stael

Week 1

Sowing
Planting
Watering
Pruning
Maintenance

February

Tip: February is a good time to trim shrubbery and climbing roses. Cut off dead branches and thin branches competing for growing space.

February

Week 3

Tip: If you have dependable local sources for seeds, plants, and materials, give them preference in your buying. They know the climatic subtleties of your area and can pass along invaluable inside advice.

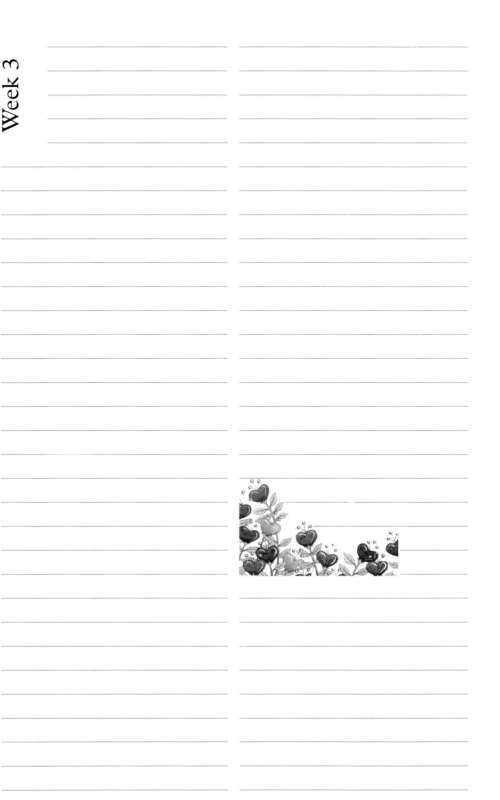

Week 4

February

Tip: Lay and repair garden paths. Fix fences. Clean pots. Organize your shed. When warm weather comes, it will be harder to find time for this kind of maintenance.

March

March will often test a gardener's patience. Warmer, brighter days will most certainly tempt you into the garden, but be cautious of starting too soon. Before you start digging, take a handful of soil and squeeze it gently. It should crumble in your hand. If the soil remains intact or falls apart in heavy clumps, it's still too wet to work. It can take several weeks of warm bright days for the soil to dry out sufficiently. As soon as it is workable, spade in manure or compost and a balanced chemical fertilizer.

On an overcast day, gradually remove the protective mulch covering from shrubs and perennials. Don't rush. Exposing young growth too quickly can mean sun and wind damage.

Week 1

Sowing
Cultivating
Pruning
Fertilizing
Planting

CLOUDS MAY COME, BUT CLOUDS MUST GO,
AND THEY HAVE A SILVER LINING,
FOR BEYOND THEM ALL, YOU KNOW,
THE SUN OR MOON IS SHINING.

March

Tip: Most plants appreciate a good meal at this season. Use a balanced fertilizer applied at the rate of four pounds per 100 square feet.

Week 2

March

Tip: Treat yourself to a sneak-preview of spring by forcing branches of flowering trees or shrubs. After their flower buds have become plump, cut branches of forsythia, azalea, pussy willow, or another early-spring bloomer. Slit or pound with a hammer the lower two inches of stem and submerge the entire branch in water for two or three hours. Place them in front of a light window and watch spring blossom!

Week 3

March

Tip: Pick pansies regularly for more blooms over a longer period.

April

Brave blooms of crocus, hyacinth, daffodil, and tulip lead the way for legions of flowers to follow. April is a celebration! Bring spring indoors with selective cuttings, but don't take too many of the leaves when you pick the blossoms—their job of making food for the bulb isn't over until they turn brown and begin to wither. When leaf buds break on roses, it's time for spring pruning. Beginning now, keep sprays or dust on roses continually.

Train your lawn to grow deep roots. Provide water and fertilizer down deep. Too much surface watering and feeding causes roots to mass near the surface. By late summer, grass without deep roots will be in deep trouble.

Week 1

Cultivating
Planting
Fertilizing
Sowing
Watering

Week 2

April

Tip: "Harden off" annuals and perennials that you have been growing inside before moving them to the garden. At first, leave them outside for only about an hour, out of direct sunlight. Over a period of about two weeks, increase the length of outdoor exposure gradually. Once hardy and acclimated, they are ready to move to their permanent home.

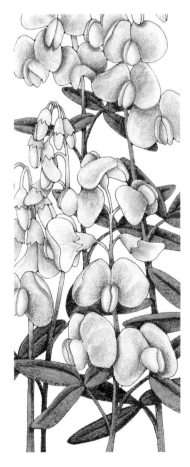

April

Tip: Fertilize perennials when they have grown to a height of two to three inches. Young flowering plants should receive frequent, light fertilization, rather than a single, heavy application. Irrigating the beds before fertilizing will help the fertilizer to penetrate the soil.

Week 3

Week 4

April

Tip: When freezing temperatures are predicted, protect tender plants by covering them with plastic or other protective material. Use a frame to hold the material away from the foliage. Heat from a light bulb placed under the protection will also help on especially cold nights.

May

In most parts of the country, May is pay-off month. Your hard work and careful planning requites itself with a show of dogwoods, magnolias, azaleas, lilacs, tulips, wild sweetwilliam, forget-me-nots, pansies, primroses, and more. Reward yourself. Get out of your own garden—visit parks, botanical gardens, nurseries, and gardens of friends and neighbors. Learn what is being grown successfully. Note striking color combinations. Share ideas. Record what you see in the section of this book titled Other People's Gardens.

Week 1

Cultivating
Planting
Fertilizing
Sowing
Watering

SILENTLY,
ONE BY ONE
IN THE INFINITE
MEADOWS
OF
HEAVEN,
BLOSSOMED THE
LOVELY STARS,
THE
FORGET-ME-NOTS
OF
ANGELS

Week 2

May

Tips: Several hours before transplanting indoor-grown seedlings, water thoroughly. This will cause soil to stick to their roots and reduce trans-plant shock when they are moved to their permanent home in the garden.

51

May

Tip: Give your house-plants a patio vacation. Move them outside for the summer. You'll be surprised at how invigorating it can be. However, be wary of over-exposing them to direct sunlight.

Week 4

May

Tip: When buying annuals, look for ones that are just beginning to bud. Plants already in flower won't have time to adapt to the growing environment of your garden.

June

For many gardeners, June means one thing— Roses! If you've planted, mulched, sprayed, dusted, pruned, and otherwise tended with loving care, you should be enjoying delicate, fragrant blooms now. If you didn't plant any and regret it, cheat! Nurseries will have a variety growing and blooming in containers, ready for easy transplant. Many will continue to bloom in your garden all summer.

Cut back perennials after they have finished flowering and use some of the growth you remove as cuttings to start new plants. Plant late-blooming, heat-resistant annuals like balsam, cosmos, marigold, gaillardia, moss-pink, morning-glory, and zinnia.

Week 1

Planting
Cultivating
Mulching
Watering
Fertilizing

June

Week 2

Tip: Conserve water, prevent weeds, and protect sensitive roots by applying two to four inches of mulch around plants and shrubs. Use compost, wood chips, manure, or peat moss. The ground should be moist and lightly cultivated before mulching.

June

Tip: By June, chrysanthemums have begun rapid growth. Encourage bushy plants and more flowers by "pinching them back," or removing their tender growing tips, about every 10 days. Continue this practice through July.

Week 3

June

Week 4

Tip: When mowing your lawn, avoid cutting more than 50 percent of the height of the grass blade. Remember, the roots are dependent on food manufactured by the leaves. When tall grass is cut short, it upsets the balance between root and leaf growth. To maintain this balance, cut grass to a uniform height, except during intense summer heat, when grass should be allowed to grow a little longer.

July

As summer sun bears down on your lawn and garden, make watering your top priority. Your garden should receive at least one inch of water per week. What Mother Nature doesn't deliver, you need to supply by garden hose. When you water, give your lawn and garden a thorough soaking—sprinkling the surface does more harm than good. Water early in the day. Moisture in mid-day is prone to evaporation and evening watering encourages leaf disease. Give lawns special attention where tree roots compete for moisture.

In central and northern areas, roses should receive their last feeding this month. This will provide them ample time to harden off tissues before the first frost.

Week 1

Watering
Fertilizing
Harvesting
Spraying
Planting

July

Week 2

Tip: To keep annuals and perennials flowering robustly over a long season, remove the flowers as they fade. Letting them go to seed reduces flower production.

July

Tip: Cut back chrysan-
themums after flowering
to encourage a second
flowering in fall.

Week 3

July

Week 4

Tip: If July is your vacation month, be sure to arrange for a neighbor or professional lawn service to water your garden and lawn. Under heat wave conditions, your lush, green landscape can become dry and brown if moisture is denied for even the shortest period.

August

Beat the August doldrums with a midsummer vegetable planting. Breathe new life into your flower beds by replacing played-out annuals with the ingredients of a fresh autumn salad. Spinach, beets, leaf lettuce, corn, escarole, endive, Chinese cabbage, brussels sprouts, and radishes are among the tasty veggies that will thrive during sunny days and crisp nights of autumn. Late summer is also a good time to divide and move perennials that tend to clump, like daylilies and iris. Discard any old, inactive portions and replant the young healthy ones. Brighten a neighbor's day by sharing extra bulbs.

Week 1

Watering
Planting
Fertilizing
Harvesting
Pest Control

August

Tip: Except in the Deep South, now is the time to order spring-flowering bulbs. Narcissus, crocus, grape hyacinth, Dutch iris, and glory-of-the-snow should be available for a late-September or early-October planting. Wait until October or November to plant tulips.

August

Tip: Don't forget the birds! They are a natural defense against many insects and an attractive compliment to your colorful flowers and trees. Furnish your garden with a birdbath and keep the water clean and fresh.

Week 3

Week 4

HOME SWEET HOME

August

Tip: Remove any dead branches from your trees before winter ice and snow storms do it for you. Dead wood is not only hazardous and unattractive, but also a host for insects and fungal diseases. Pruning now provides trees ample time for cambium growth before cold sets in.

September

As activity in the garden slows, it's time to "winterize" your lawn. Remove thatch and matted grass to provide room for new growth and to allow ample air and moisture to reach grass plants. If your lawn has become compacted from heavy foot-traffic this summer, have it aerated. Where needed, reseed your lawn by hand or with a seed spreader. After seeding, water well to work seeds into the soil. Fertilize your lawn in September to encourage a fall recovery after summer's damaging heat and drought. This is also a good month to transplant dormant perennials. Wait for a cloudy day, and move them with a ball of earth around the roots.

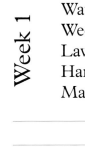

Week 1

Watering
Weeding
Lawn Care
Harvesting
Maintenance

Week 2

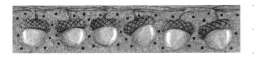

September

Tip: With their summer growth phase completed, now is a good time to plant or transplant evergreens. Keep well-watered after planting.

September

Tip: Pumpkins and squash should be harvested before they are nipped by frost. Cure them in the sun for two weeks, and then store them in a cool, dry place. Handle carefully to avoid bruising and cutting.

Week 3

Week 4

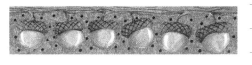

September

Tip: Before the first frost, harvest any full-size green tomatoes remaining on the vine. Wrap them individually in newspaper and put them in a cool, humid place (85-90 percent humidity is ideal). The cooler the location, the slower the fruit will ripen, but never store them where the temperature is below 54° or they'll have inferior flavor.

October

Shorter days and colder nights of October usher in the arm-chair gardening season for many people, but a few hours outside among the falling leaves will pay great dividends next spring (and keep your cheeks rosy). Remove any remaining dead plants from your garden, rake up leaves, and trim your lawn. Unless this foliage shows signs of disease or insect infestation, you can work it directly into your garden plot where it will decompose and enrich the soil. Also add a balanced chemical fertilizer. Leave the ground rough over the winter and it will catch and retain more moisture. Don't neglect your roses! To ward off pests and disease, they should be sprayed or dusted as long as they are in active growth. Now is the time to order new roses for November planting.

Week 1

Clean-up
Ordering
Harvesting
Planting
Watering

Week 2

October

Tip: After frost has killed their foliage, dig out bulbs of amaryllis, cannas, dahlias, gladioli, caladium, and tuberous begonias. Dry bulbs in the sun for a few hours and then store them in a cool, dry place for the winter. Always dig bulbs rather than pull them out by their foliage.

October

Tip: In climates where they will have ample time to establish themselves before really cold weather sets in, October is an excellent month to plant most deciduous trees and shrubs.

Week 3

October

Week 4

Tip: Birds are among the gardener's best friends. Tempt them to visit and encourage them to stay by hanging bird feeders, suet racks, and feeding boxes. Be consistent in your feeding, especially in the coming winter months when snow may cover their natural food sources.

November

The cold air of November means it's time to "tuck in" your perennials before harsh winter weather arrives. Just before the ground freezes hard, hill up soil around the base of rose bushes and climbing roses to a height of six to eight inches. Tie rose branches loosely with strips of cloth to prevent them from being whipped by winter winds. Protect roses as well as newly planted tulips and other spring-flowering bulbs by covering them with a heavy layer of mulch—the colder your winter climate, the thicker your mulch should be. Mulch will keep the soil warmer in the fall and prevent it from warming up too quickly in spring.

Week 1

Mulching
Pruning
Clean-up
Ordering
Maintenance

Week 2

November

Tip: Clean and store garden tools and machinery. Wipe metal blades with oil to prevent rust. If power equipment like lawn mowers and soil tillers need servicing, take care of them now rather than in spring when repair shops will be backlogged.

November

Tip: Finish any planting
of spring-flowering bulbs
as soon as possible.

Week 3

Week 4

November

Tip: When fall planting is finished, shut off and drain all outside water lines to pools and garden areas. Turn off the water to outside faucets, too, and avoid a plumber's bill for ruptured pipes.

December

Although in most regions plant growth will be held to a standstill, shrubs and trees will still appreciate an occasional watering. If unseasonably mild temperatures keep the ground from freezing, water them early in the day. However, don't water so frequently that you force new growth—once every three weeks should be adequate.

If you plan to add an evergreen tree to your landscape, consider buying a living Christmas tree from a nursery. Many varieties of spruce, fir, and pine are good candidates. You can keep the potted tree indoors for up to two weeks. As soon as possible after Christmas, move it to a sheltered spot outdoors, and give it about a week to acclimate before planting.

Week 1

Ordering
Planning
Maintenance
Clean-up
Watering

Week 2

December

Tip: Don't discard your Christmas tree after the holiday season ends. Instead, add its boughs to the mulch protecting perennials and low-growing evergreens.

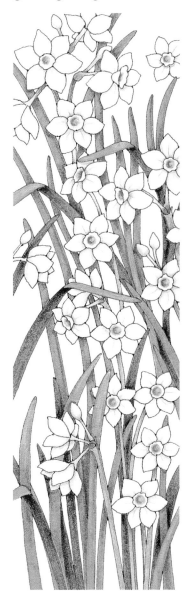

December

Tip: Check stored bulbs to make sure they are wintering well. If stored under dry and cool (45 - 55°) conditions, bulbs should stay plump and firm.

Week 3

Week 4

December

Tip: Put your Christmas poinsettia in a warm, sunny spot where the temperature remains constant and doesn't drop below 60° at night. When leaves begin to fall off in late winter or early spring, move the plant into partial darkness and water lightly once a week. After the danger of frost is past, cut the stems back to within four inches of the soil, repot, and plant it, pot and all, in a sunny spot outside. Cuttings taken from your plant in June or July should produce Christmas flowers next year.

Plantings Record

All plants need sunlight, moisture, and food to survive, but beyond these general requirements, different types of plants can have significantly different needs. The more variety your garden holds, the harder it is to keep track of these specific needs. The Records section that follows should help you with this task.

The Records section is divided into nine categories which include the major sub-groups of lawn and garden plant life: trees and shrubs, grass, annuals, perennials, roses, bulbs, vegetables and herbs, fruit, and potted plants. For each of these categories, two to four lined pages are provided for detailed record-keeping. Think of this section as your landscape's inventory list. When completed, every growing thing on your lawn and in your garden (except weeds) should be included somewhere in this section.

To help guide you in your record-keeping, a checklist appears at the beginning of each Records section. This checklist will remind you of important information to record like supplier, date planted, location planted, blooming date, and feeding, pruning, and spraying schedules.

The Records section will be especially valuable when used in tandem with the garden grids in the Taking Stock section of this book. Once completed, every item in the Records section should also appear on your Current Garden Grid on pages 12 and 13. By referring to your grid, you'll be able to see, graphically, the position and exposure of each plant.

Trees & Shrubs

When choosing a tree or shrub to plant, keep in mind both your local climate and your reasons for wanting the tree or shrub. Do you want summer shade? Spring flowers? Colorful fall foliage? A fast-growing species? Something to provide privacy or block the wind? Do you prefer evergreens or deciduous trees? Be sure to consider how large the tree will be at maturity, and make certain both the branches and the roots will have ample growing room. Trees will be the most permanent and dominant residents of your yard or garden, so explore all the possibilities and choose carefully.

Name
Supplier
Date Planted
Location/Conditions
Height, Color, Ornamentals
Feeding, Pruning, Spraying
Problems

Trees & Shrubs

Tip: After planting a tree, wrap its trunk and major branches with burlap or another protective material. This will protect the tree from borers and weather damage.

Grass & Lawn

Choose a grass that fits your climate. Grasses fall into two general categories. Cool-season grasses, which include bluegrass, fescues, and bents, grow best in the northern part of the country. Warm-season grasses, like zoysias, bermudas, and St. Augustine, prefer the South. In central states, go with what works best locally. Some grasses require considerably more maintenance than others—consider this *before* planting. Once established, maintaining a lush, green lawn depends on fertilization, weed control, and consistent mowing. Begin mowing early in spring, as soon as grass begins to grow, and continue until it becomes dormant.

Type of Grass
Dates Planted
Dates Fertilized
Aerated/Dethatched
Mowing
Weed Control

Grass & Lawn

Tip: Should you let grass clippings lie after mowing? It depends—mainly on your grass type. With lawns like Kentucky bluegrass or fescue, which grow in a fairly open manner, cut grass will usually settle into the soil and decompose, aiding fertility. The density of grasses like bermuda and zoysia, however, doesn't allow clippings to reach the soil level. Clippings of these types of grasses should be collected.

Annuals

Whether providing a quick dash of color, lining a garden path, or beautifying space until perennials take hold, annuals are versatile garden do-it-alls. Annuals are plants that complete their entire life cycle in one season. Novice and expert gardeners alike love annuals for the ease with which they can be planted and grown. Annual seeds can be sown directly into the ground or planted indoors and moved when frost-danger is past. Popular annuals include zinnias, marigolds, petunias, and ageratums, but the tremendous variety of other annuals allows you to match your plantings to your individual preference and personality. In general, annuals love sunshine and will grow in any type of soil if well tended and fertilized.

Name

Supplier

Location/Conditions

Date Planted

Flowering Date

Height/Color

Problems

Annuals

Tip: The goal of annuals is seed production, which is accomplished through flowering. By picking faded flowers off of annuals before seeds ripen, you can extend their flowering season until freezing temperatures set in.

Perennials

If annuals are the spotlighted soloists of the garden concerto, perennials are the reliable, indispensible orchestra. Perennials are flowering or foliage plants which bloom year after year—some, in fact, may outlive you! In cold winter climates, the tops of perennials die at the end of the growing season, but the dormant roots store food and produce new plants the following spring. Generally, perennials develop more slowly than annuals, and most don't begin to bloom robustly until their second growing season, but once established, they will become the backbone of your garden sceme. Hollyhock, alyssum, delphinium, lupine, phlox, and primrose are among the most popular perennials.

Name
Supplier
Location/Conditions
Date Planted
Flowering Date
Height/Color
Problems

Perennials

Tip: Just because they are loyal and dependable bloomers, don't neglect established perennials. Many varieties will benefit from being dug up, divided, and replanted every few years.

Roses

Roses are the royalty of garden flora. America's favorite flower can be successfully grown in nearly any climate—and cultivating the perfect bloom is a consuming passion for gardeners everywhere. The rose's popularity has given rise to thousands of varieties, and new hybrids are constantly being developed. Roses are sold three ways: bare-root, packaged, and potted. A healthy, dormant bare-root plant is probably your best bet. Spring planting is advisable in colder regions, but in most areas, plants can be set out in spring or fall. Potted plants give you the option of summertime planting, but be wary of plants whose roots have become potbound.

Name/Type

Supplier

Date Planted

Location/Conditions

Feeding/Spraying/Dusting

Pruning

Flowering Date

Color/Height

Problems

Roses

Tip: Plant roses in narrow beds (no more than 4-5 feet wide) to make them accessible for tending and picking. Plants should be set in full sunlight 2-3 feet apart and as far away as possible from large shrubs and trees whose roots would compete for moisture.

Bulbs

The bells of hyacinth, the trumpets of daffodil, and an ensemble of other spring-blooming bulb flowers herald the arrival of a new growing season with vigorous growth and glorious colors. Bulbs are nature's self-contained flower production kits—inside a dormant bulb resides either a fully-formed flower bud or a supply of food available to give the flower a boost through the warming soil of spring. The foliage of bulb flowers performs the critical function of food production, so the more foliage a plant has, the more food will be stored for next year's bloom. After blooms have died or been cut, let its leaves continue to grow until they have withered or turned brown.

Name
Supplier
Date Planted
Location/Depth Planted
Flowering Date
Color/Height
Problems

Bulbs

Tip: Proper soil preparation is a key to bulb performance. Soil should be deeply cultivated and contain plenty of organic material. Soil should also be moist—especially the soil below the bulb where roots will grow. Make sure bulbs are in good contact with the soil; air space around the bulb can kill it.

Vegetables & Herbs

The incomparable taste of homegrown vegetables and the satisfaction of producing your own food make vegetable gardening a labor of love for millions. To produce fresh vegetables and herbs for your dinner table all you need is a plot of relatively good, well-drained soil in full sunlight, away from the shade and root networks of trees and shrubs. For more fragrant herbs, plant them in sandy soil. By rotating cool-weather growers like broccoli, cauliflower, lettuce, carrots, peas, beets, and radishes with warm-weather vegetables like tomatoes, beans, squash, peppers, corn, and cucumbers, you can harvest fresh food from spring to late autumn.

Name
Supplier
Date Planted
Location/Conditions
Harvesting Date
Quality/Quantity
Problems

Vegetables & Herbs

Tip: If your garden plot is small, maximize productivity by planting vegetables that require less growing space. Broccoli, lettuce, onions, spinach, beans, peppers, carrots, and tomatoes are among those that produce lots of food in tight quarters.

Fruit

What a treat to pick and eat a piece of ripe, juicy fruit in your own backyard! Fruit gardening can be extremely rewarding, but doing a little homework before you plant will save frustration and expense. Many fruits are highly climate sensitive. To determine which fruits offer the best prospects for your area, seek the advice of local nurseries. Some fruit-bearing trees and bushes are picky about soil makeup, so consider having yours tested. Once you've determined what will thrive in your climate, consider the space you're willing to commit to the pursuit of fruit. All fruit-bearing plants need attention if they are to produce sweet rewards, so be prepared to invest your time and labor.

Name/Type
Supplier
Date Planted
Location/Conditions
Flowering Date
Feeding, Pruning, Spraying
Problems

Fruit

Tip: Dwarf trees give you all the benefits of a full-sized fruit tree, but make pruning, spraying, and picking easier and less expensive. Dwarf trees are created by grafting fruit trees onto growth-inhibiting root systems. Plant dwarf trees at a depth where the graft union is a few inches above the soil line so that roots don't form above the union and spoil the dwarfing effect.

Potted Plants

Container-grown plants can be a significant and versatile component of your outdoor and indoor landscapes. Whether planted in a clay pot, half barrel, or homemade wooden box, a potted plant's greatest asset is mobility. Remember, container-grown plants dry out much faster then their earthbound cousins and need to be watered more often. In general, container-grown plants should be watered thoroughly and then let dry almost completely before rewatering. Water must be able to drain from the container or roots are likely to rot. Because they lack access to earth's nutrient sources, potted plants should also be fed frequently.

Types Planted
Locations
Date Set Out
Flowering Date
Color
Problems

Potted Plants

Tip: When building flower boxes, use a rot-resistant wood like redwood or cedar. Boards should be 1 inch thick to prevent warping, and they should be fastened with screws instead of nails which tend to pop out under the strain of soil and water. Remember, always drill holes in the bottom for water drainage and make certain they are kept unclogged.

Other People's Gardens

There's always work to be done in the garden, but when you're caught up with the big chores, or when you just need a little break, treat yourself to a peek at someone else's horticultural handiwork. Bring this book along when you visit botanical gardens, flower shows, public gardens, and gardens of friends and neighbors. Use this section to record which gardens you have visited, unique layouts, unusual plants or presentation, striking color combinations, and overall impressions. Strike up conversations and pay attention to the details— you never know where your next great garden idea will come from!

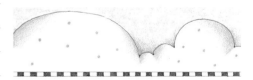

General Reference

Major Types of Roses

Type	Comments
Hybrid tea	Long-pointed buds and large flowers Blooms grow one to a stem on 3-6 foot plants Excellent for cutting (the "florist's" rose)
Floribunda	Well-formed buds and flowers (like tea, but smaller) Hardy growers that flower in clusters Bloom continuously and profusely
Polyantha	Bloom intermittently on small bushes Clusters of small flowers "Old" species which has been largely replaced by floribunda
Grandiflora	Descendant from hybrid tea and floribunda Large flowers usually grow several to a stem Vigorous growers which often grow very tall
Climbers	Usually large blossomed—flowers similar to hybrid tea Most varieties are ever-blooming Don't really climb, but produce limber canes which can be attached to a trellis or support

How to Plant a Tree

Dig a hole that is at least one foot wider and deeper than the size of the tree's root system. Fill the hole to the top with water and let it drain. When it has drained, fill it again. It should drain again within an hour, but it may take longer. If it takes more than 12 hours to empty, drainage is too slow and you should probably plant elsewhere.

Once you've found a spot with proper drainage, loosen the earth in the bottom of the hole and mix in good topsoil and moistened peat moss.

Place the tree in the hole at a depth where the soil line is the same as it was when the tree was in the nursery or its container. Fill in the hole with the best soil available. Mix in peat moss and a complete plant food. The best soil should be at the bottom. Firm the soil. When the hole is almost filled, water thoroughly and then complete filling.

It will usually take six months to a year for the tree to get truly established and for its roots to start functioning well.

Tips for Cutting Flowers

- The best time to pick flowers is early in the morning or in the evening after sundown. (Exception: Roses should be picked in mid-afternoon.)

- Select flowers that have recently bloomed or are in late bud stage.

- Submerge stems in lukewarm water immediately after cutting.

- Cut at a slant to maximize the area through which water can be taken in.

- Don't take more leaves than necessary—they're needed to make food.

- Remove all foliage below the waterline.

- Slit or pound the lower 2-3 inches of woody-stemmed plants to facilitate water absorption.

Pruning Tips

Proper pruning of trees and shrubs improves their health and appearance, controls size and shape, and increases flower production. Here are some basic tips:

- Cut out dead, diseased, or damaged wood that interferes with new growth. When cutting away dead wood, make pruning cut an inch or two into the live, healthy wood.

- When removing branches or twigs, make the cut flush with the side of the trunk or branch to which it is attached. Don't leave a stub.

- To change the shape of a plant, cut it back to where a bud or branch grows in the direction you want the plant to grow.

- When pruning back to a bud, make the cut at a slight slant about 1/4 inch beyond the top of the bud (see page 106). Generally, the bud should be pointing outward, rather than to the center of the plant.

- When two branches cross or rub against one another, remove the smaller, weaker one.

- Make sure pruning cuts are smooth and clean.

- If the diameter of the branch cut is an inch or more, apply a tree wound dressing.

Cutting & Pruning Tips

Pruning & Planting

Proper Pruning Angle

Right   **Wrong**

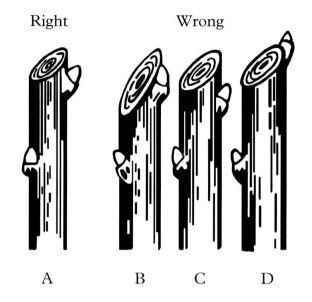

A   B   C   D

When possible, cut back to a side bud and make the cut at a slant. *A* is cut correctly. *B* is too slanting. *C* is too far from the bud. *D* is too close to the bud.

Bulb Planting Depth

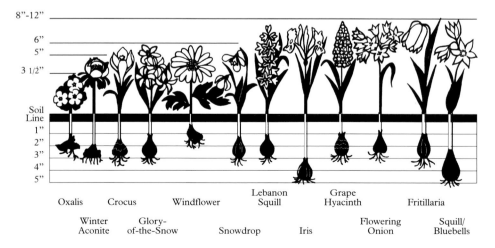

Oxalis   Crocus   Windflower   Lebanon Squill   Grape Hyacinth   Fritillaria

Winter Aconite   Glory-of-the-Snow   Snowdrop   Iris   Flowering Onion   Squill/Bluebells

Frost-safe Dates

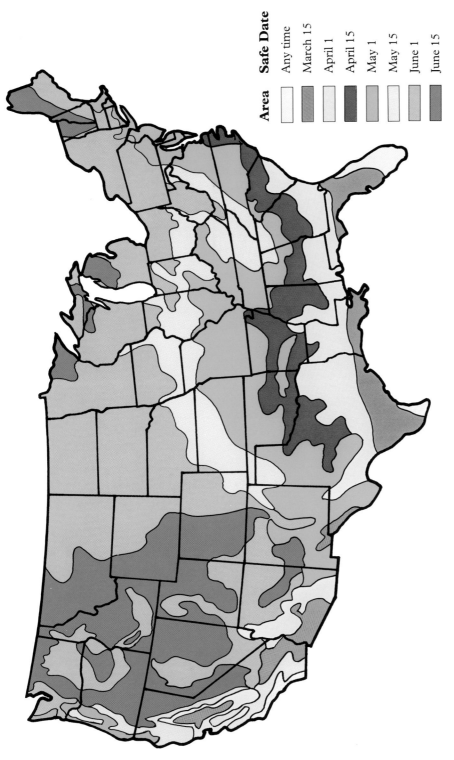

Area	Safe Date
	Any time
	March 15
	April 1
	April 15
	May 1
	May 15
	June 1
	June 15

Planting & Conversion

Vegetable Planting

Cold-hardy plants for early-spring planting		Cold-tender or heat-hardy plants for late-spring or early-summer planting			Hardy plants for late-summer or fall planting except in the North (plant 6 to 8 weeks before first fall freeze)
Very hardy (plant 4 to 6 weeks before frost-free date)	Hardy (plant 2 to 4 weeks before frost-free date)	Not cold-hardy (plant on frost-free date)	Requiring hot weather (plant 1 week or more after frost-free date)	Medium heat-tolerant (good for summer planting)	
Broccoli Cabbage Lettuce Onions Peas Potato Spinach Turnip	Beets Carrot Chard Mustard Parsnip Radish	Beans-snap Okra Soybean Squash Sweet corn Tomato	Beans-lima Eggplant Peppers Sweet potato Cucumber Melons	Beans Soybean Squash Sweet corn	Beets Collard Kale Lettuce Mustard Spinach Turnip

Conversion Table

To convert	to	multiply by:
centimeters	feet	0.03
centimeters	inches	0.39
cubic cm	cubin in.	0.06
cubic ft.	cubic m	0.03
feet	cm	30.48
gallons	liters	3.79
gal. water	lb. water	8.35
grams	ounces	0.04
inches	cm	2.54
kilograms	pounds	2.21
kilometers	feet	3,280.80
kilometers	miles	0.62
liters	gallons	0.26
liters	pints	2.11
meters	feet	3.28
ounces	grams	28.35
pounds	kg	0.45

Fluid Volume

1 tablespoon (tbs.) = 3 teaspoons (tsp.)
= 0.5 fluid ounce (fl. oz.)
1 cup = 8 fl. oz.
1 pint (pt.) = 2 cups = 16 fl. oz.
1 quart (qt.) = 2 pt. = 4 cups
= 32 fl. oz.
1 gallon (gal.) = 4 qt. = 8 pt. = 16 cups
1 bushel (bu.) = 8 gal. = 32 qt.

Conversions
1 fluid ounce = 29.57 ml = 0.03 L
1 cup = 236.59 ml = 0.24 L
1 pint = 473.18 ml = 0.47 L
1 quart = 946.35 ml
= 0.95 L
1 gallon = 3,785.41 ml = 3.79 L
1 milliliter = 0.03 fluid ounce
1 liter = 33.81 fluid ounces
= 4.23 cups = 2.11 pints
= 1.06 quarts = 0.26 gallons

Length or Distance

1 foot (ft.) = 12 inches (in.)
1 yard (yd.) = 3 ft. = 36 in.
1 mile = 1,760 yd. = 5,280 ft.

Conversions
1 in. = 2.54 cm = 0.03 m
1 ft. = 30.48 cm = 0.30 m
1 yd. = 91.44 cm = 0.91 m
1 mi. = 1,609.34 m
= 1.61 km
1 cm = 0.39 in.
1 m = 1.09 yd.
= 3.28 ft.

Measures

Supplier
Names

Name_____
    Address_____
    Phone_____
    Contact_____
    Supplier of_____

Name_____
    Address_____
    Phone_____
    Contact_____
    Supplier of_____

Name_____
    Address_____
    Phone_____
    Contact_____
    Supplier of_____

Name_____
    Address_____
    Phone_____
    Contact_____
    Supplier of_____

Name_____
    Address_____
    Phone_____
    Contact_____
    Supplier of_____

Name_____
    Address_____
    Phone_____
    Contact_____
    Supplier of_____

Name_____
    Address_____
    Phone_____
    Contact_____
    Supplier of_____

Name_____
    Address_____
    Phone_____
    Contact_____
    Supplier of_____

Name_____
    Address_____
    Phone_____
    Contact_____
    Supplier of_____

Name_____
    Address_____
    Phone_____
    Contact_____
    Supplier of_____

Name_____   Name_____
   Address_____   Address_____
   Phone_____   Phone_____
   Contact_____   Contact_____
   Supplier of_____   Supplier of_____

Name_____   Name_____
   Address_____   Address_____
   Phone_____   Phone_____
   Contact_____   Contact_____
   Supplier of_____   Supplier of_____

Name_____   Name_____
   Address_____   Address_____
   Phone_____   Phone_____
   Contact_____   Contact_____
   Supplier of_____   Supplier of_____

Name_____   Name_____
   Address_____   Address_____
   Phone_____   Phone_____
   Contact_____   Contact_____
   Supplier of_____   Supplier of_____

Name_____   Name_____
   Address_____   Address_____
   Phone_____   Phone_____
   Contact_____   Contact_____
   Supplier of_____   Supplier of_____

Notes